To be born again as a man is not easy.

Buddha said it was as rare as for a

single one-eyed turtle that swims beneath

the surface of the oceans to emerge into

the air, once every hundred years,

by passing its head through the collar of

an ox-yoke adrift in the vast ocean.

For Danielle, without whom Zanskar would not be quite so beautiful ...

Olivier

Translated from the French
Si loin des Hommes si près des Dieux
by Jane Brenton

'A Journey of Initiation' was first published (in French)
in Olivier Föllmi's *Deux hivers au Zanskar*. Éditions
Olizane, Geneva, 1983. Reproduced with kind
permission of the publishers.

'The Road to Enlightenment' was first published
(in French) in Olivier Föllmi's *Caravane pour une école*.
Éditions Nathan, Paris, 1990 (Éditions de La Martinière,
Paris, 1993).

This edition first published in the United Kingdom in
1999 by Thames & Hudson Ltd, 181A High Holborn,
London WC1V 7QX

First published in hardback in the United States
of America in 1999 by Thames & Hudson Inc.,
500 Fifth Avenue, New York, New York 10110

British Library Cataloguing-in-Publication Data
A catalogue record for this book is available from
the British Library

Library of Congress Catalog Card Number 99-070950

ISBN 0-500-01954-1

Printed and bound in Switzerland

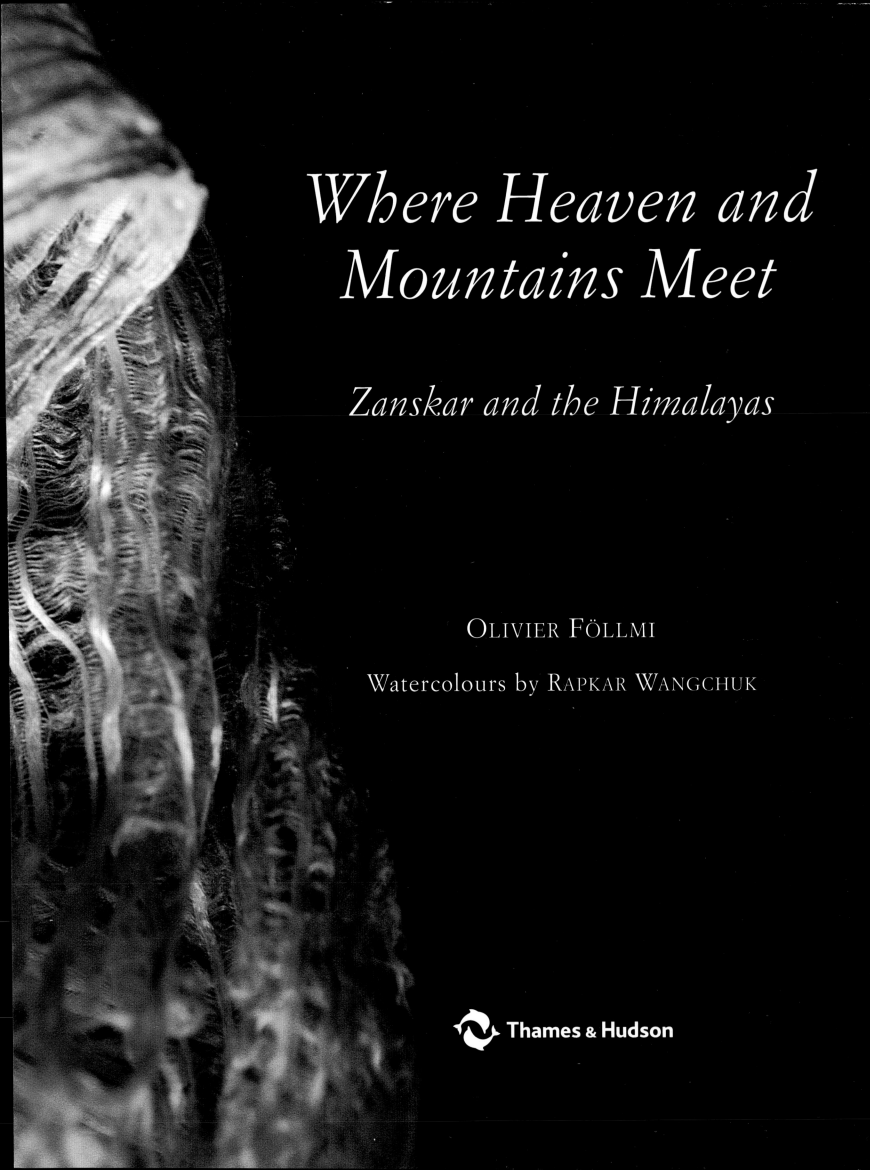

Where Heaven and Mountains Meet

Zanskar and the Himalayas

OLIVIER FÖLLMI

Watercolours by RAPKAR WANGCHUK

Thames & Hudson

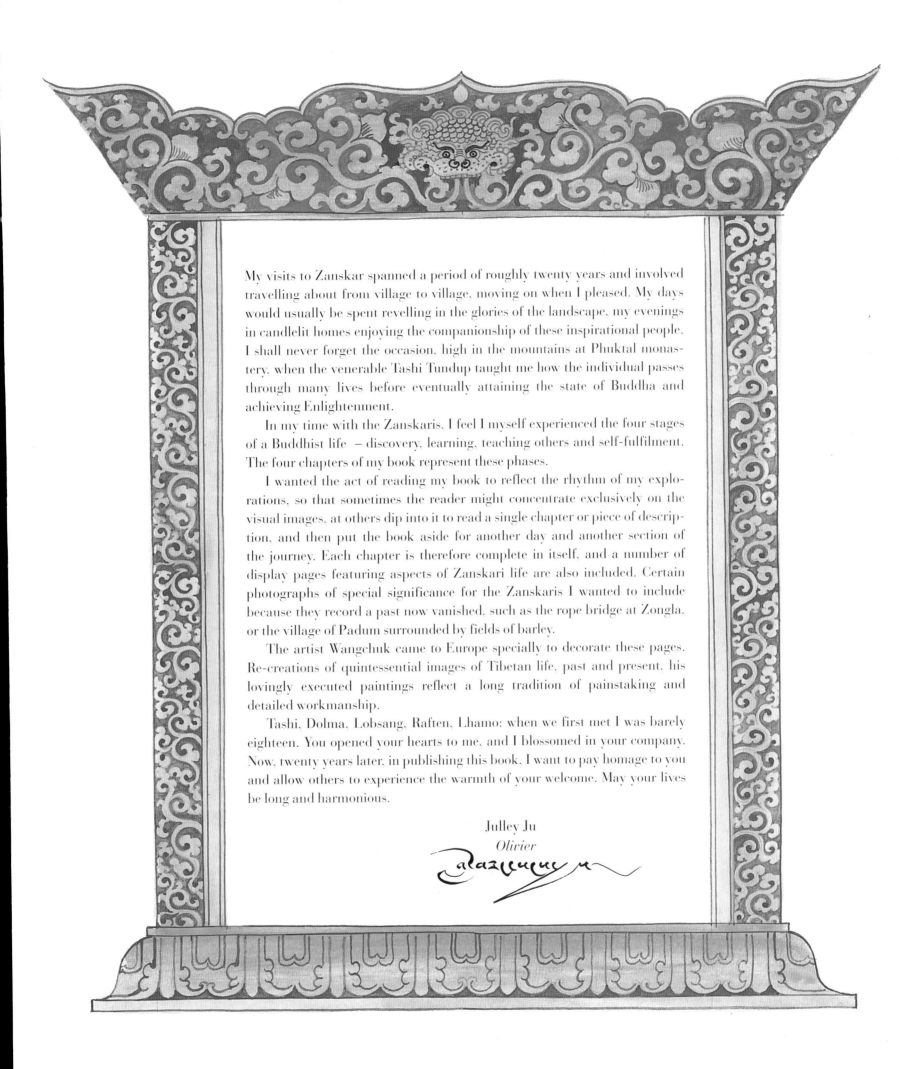

My visits to Zanskar spanned a period of roughly twenty years and involved travelling about from village to village, moving on when I pleased. My days would usually be spent revelling in the glories of the landscape, my evenings in candlelit homes enjoying the companionship of these inspirational people. I shall never forget the occasion, high in the mountains at Phuktal monastery, when the venerable Tashi Tundup taught me how the individual passes through many lives before eventually attaining the state of Buddha and achieving Enlightenment.

In my time with the Zanskaris, I feel I myself experienced the four stages of a Buddhist life – discovery, learning, teaching others and self-fulfilment. The four chapters of my book represent these phases.

I wanted the act of reading my book to reflect the rhythm of my explorations, so that sometimes the reader might concentrate exclusively on the visual images, at others dip into it to read a single chapter or piece of description, and then put the book aside for another day and another section of the journey. Each chapter is therefore complete in itself, and a number of display pages featuring aspects of Zanskari life are also included. Certain photographs of special significance for the Zanskaris I wanted to include because they record a past now vanished, such as the rope bridge at Zongla, or the village of Padum surrounded by fields of barley.

The artist Wangchuk came to Europe specially to decorate these pages. Re-creations of quintessential images of Tibetan life, past and present, his lovingly executed paintings reflect a long tradition of painstaking and detailed workmanship.

Tashi, Dolma, Lobsang, Raften, Lhamo: when we first met I was barely eighteen. You opened your hearts to me, and I blossomed in your company. Now, twenty years later, in publishing this book, I want to pay homage to you and allow others to experience the warmth of your welcome. May your lives be long and harmonious.

Julley Ju

Olivier

A FATHER'S LOVE

In October, some Zanskaris go to Lahaul or follow the Jumlam route to Ladakh, taking advantage of the brief period after the harvest is over and before the winter sets in. Their purpose is to barter butter and wool in exchange for a small metal cooking stove, to make life in winter more agreeable, or for spices to enliven their meals of barley flour. Sonam Norboo took his seven-year-old son to Manali to have an eye infection treated. It took a week's walking to get there, and the doctor gave the boy eye drops. On the way back to Zanskar, at the foot of the Shing Kun La, at 5,100 metres (16,700 feet), a snowstorm blew up. It continued for three days. The boy followed behind his father until the snow was too deep for him to walk. Then his father carried him on his shoulders, protecting him from the elements with a blanket, the ends of which he clasped to his chest. Walking straight into the icy wind, Sonam Norboo developed frostbite in his exposed hands and lost all his fingers. The boy, however, was cured.

THE ROAD TO WISDOM

Buddhists regard anger as a sign of weakness, and no one ever shouts or loses his temper in Zanskar. Passion is discouraged and nothing is ever expressed in terms of strong emotion. From childhood onwards, individuals are taught to rein in their impulses. They may feel resentment, but must never let it become hatred. Joy is always to be tempered with restraint. The aim of each individual is to develop an inner peace that will enable him to gain an understanding of the holy texts. The social ideal is the renunciation of material goods and the rule of self, in order to escape the prison of a body and spirit overly attached to this world. Only when these goals have been achieved is it possible to apprehend a more universal truth. It is in developing the capacity for love, Buddhists believe, that each of us will be brought closer to our fellow beings and to all other living creatures.

INDUS

Leh
3500 M

Kanda La
4900 M

Markha

Nang Au La
5200 M

Tcharchar La
5000 M

Rangdum Gompa

Zongla
3400 M

Karcha

Raru

Padum
3500 M

Phuktal
Gompa

Ichar

Surle

ZANSKAR

N

Testa
4000 M

Karsyag

Shing Kun La
5100 M

In mid-March, I decided to go up Lung Nak, the 'Black Valley', to visit Phuktal, the most remote and spectacular of Zanskar's monasteries, situated at an altitude of 4,000 metres (13,000 feet) and supporting a community of some fifty monks. My travelling companions were my old friends Lobsang and Norboo. Ours was the last caravan of the year to pass along the frost-bound river. The thaw was imminent and we had to test the thin covering of ice with a stick at regular intervals. For five days we picked our way cautiously over the slush. We were royally entertained in the villages we passed through – Mine, Raru and Surle – and spent lively evenings drinking the local *chang* in smoky winter rooms. *Chang* is an alcoholic drink much favoured by the Zanskaris. Made from fermented barley grain, in taste and alcoholic content it greatly resembles cider. The Zanskaris love making merry; if the harvest has been good and there are sufficient reserves of barley, they are inclined to celebrate all winter long, moving on from one house to the next. But my heart was no longer in it. The unvarying diet of barley flour and greasy butter tea had sapped my strength. For weeks I had been walking over frozen rivers and I had become so thoroughly assimilated into the life here that I was losing touch with my Western roots. I missed my family acutely. Danielle and I had not had news of each other since my departure five months earlier.

There was still no route out of Zanskar: the river was thawing and the passes were deep in snow. It would be two months before I could hope to begin the long journey over the cols, at night, across frozen snow. When I had set out originally, I craved this simple but happy life. Now I was desperate to return to a milder climate and an easier existence. And I longed for female company.

ༀ་ མཛའ་བའི་མཉེན་ལོག་སྒྱུ་།།ལ་

MARRIED LOVE

It is unusual for young Zanskaris to marry for love. Falling in love is much too chancy a basis for a shared life. Instead, the parents choose their children's spouses. A young man will be happy to defer to his parents' experience in the matter, as they are bound to have a better idea of what makes for a good marriage, having already encountered the problems the new couple will face when the children are born, at harvest time, and during a harsh winter. They also know what it means to grow old. They can anticipate the difficulties that lie in wait for the young couple. In seeking a good match for their son, parents will look to families of equal wealth to their own, hoping to find a girl with a similar upbringing. Mutual tolerance will help the young couple adapt, even though they have never met before. Living together will teach them love and respect. The birth of a child, a good harvest, difficulties overcome, offerings to the monks – these are the milestones that create love and happiness within the family.

A yak grazing outside Testa, in spring. ⚜⚜

It was an old monk in Trangse who taught me that there is an art to dying. Having passed his whole life at Phuktal monastery, he had gone back to his village to await death in the bosom of his family. Wrapped in a thick goatskin coat, he would spend his days praying in a dark room. He spoke very little, but what he did say was always loving, never judgmental. An aura seemed to emanate from him in that shadowy room and, without thinking, I picked up a rosary and began saying prayers, absorbing words of wisdom that gradually surfaced in my conscious mind as self-evident truths. In a moment of insight, I understood that if I wanted to explore the spiritual world, I needed to change my life now, or I would grow old and die having wasted myself in material pursuits. As I saw the effort it would take to conquer my lazy and hedonistic instincts, I was filled with admiration for the old monk's ability to subdue his desires. Threading the beads of the rosary through my fingers, I remember feeling that I had been given a pearl beyond price. Alas, wisdom comes only with time and perseverance. My prayers were heartfelt as I told my rosary, but I was surprised to find my thoughts straying to the next stage of my journey and to the recollection of past happinesses. Easier for me, it seemed, to shoulder my backpack and probe the depths of a river than to probe my own soul. I had no wish to return to the populated world of the plains, but I did not possess this man's willpower and discipline. Although I knew deep down that he, in his poverty, held the key to true happiness.

This old monk was spending his last days praying with his family in the village of Trangse. Note the prayer wheel to the right of the picture.

At the beginning of the century, in Tibet, there lived a guru named Mipham.
He was a sort of Leonardo da Vinci of the Himalayas.
It is said of him that he invented the clock, the cannon and the aeroplane.
Every time he had finished one of his inventions,
he destroyed it,
saying it would only be another distraction.

The Frozen River

Lobsang and Dolma are a Zanskari peasant couple with whom Danielle and I have become great friends during the fifteen or so years that we have known one another. When we first met, they, like us, were recently married. Their son, Motup, was three, and Diskit just a baby. One summer, Lobsang lost his horse, and with it his livelihood, and I helped him buy another. The following winter, out on the Tchadar, or Frozen River (as they call the Zanskar Sangpo), he saved my life. With each passing year, the pattern of our lives became increasingly interwoven, and the affection between us grew.

One summer's day, in 1987, when the harvest was in, I suggested to Lobsang that we visit the Indian plains. On horseback, we crossed the Great Himalayan Range via the Shing Kun La, at 5,100 metres (16,700 feet). It took the best part of two weeks to reach the hamlet of Darcha, and from there we went by ramshackle bus to Manali, and thence to the city of Chandigarh. Lobsang was entranced by the pine trees and flowers, and in the bustling streets of the bazaars was introduced to the miracles of the twentieth century: a bicycle, a mail box, an electric light bulb, a public tap, a fruit stall. He was like a child at Christmas, lost in wonder. What it

Returning to Zanskar along the Tchadar (or Frozen River).

brought home to him above all was the remoteness of Zanskar. Back in his own land, he regretfully concluded he was too old to explore this magical new world, but he was determined to give his son Motup, then aged eight, the chance. The best solution seemed for Danielle and me to enrol him in a good school, the nearest being in Leh, 150 kilometres (more than 90 miles) away in the Ladakh Valley. That autumn, Lobsang escorted his son over the Jumlam passes to the Lamdon Model School, a respected Buddhist educational establishment, privately run, where Motup would learn Tibetan, English, Hindi and general science. For three years he remained there as a boarder, unable to visit his family. In summer, Motup's parents were too busy in the fields to fetch him, and during his long winter vacation the only passable route was the Frozen River. Although Zanskar is cut off by snows for nine months of the year, during January and February the Zanskar Sangpo is covered with thick ice, and it is possible to walk to Ladakh in a little over a week. In practice, the route is hazardous and little used, as the river flows for much of its length between the walls of a narrow ravine. Twice a year, Danielle and I acted as intermediaries between Motup in his school and his parents in Zanskar. Motup loved his studies and was a brilliant pupil, but he was only eleven, and after three years away he missed his family badly. The longing in his eyes was unmistakable one day when we brought him a slab of hard cheese from home.

The four of us talked and we determined to bring Motup back over the Frozen River to Zanskar for his next winter vacation. It was agreed that Lobsang would set off down the river in early January, accompanied by some strong men from the village, and that we would all meet up at the school in Ladakh and return together with Motup. We would later escort him back to school before the ice melted. The plan we hatched by the glow of a candle filled us with delight at the prospect of all meeting up again in the coming winter. After an exchange of *kataks*, we said emotional farewells. (*Kataks* are white scarves, offered to a god or an individual.

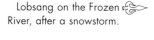

Lobsang on the Frozen River, after a snowstorm.

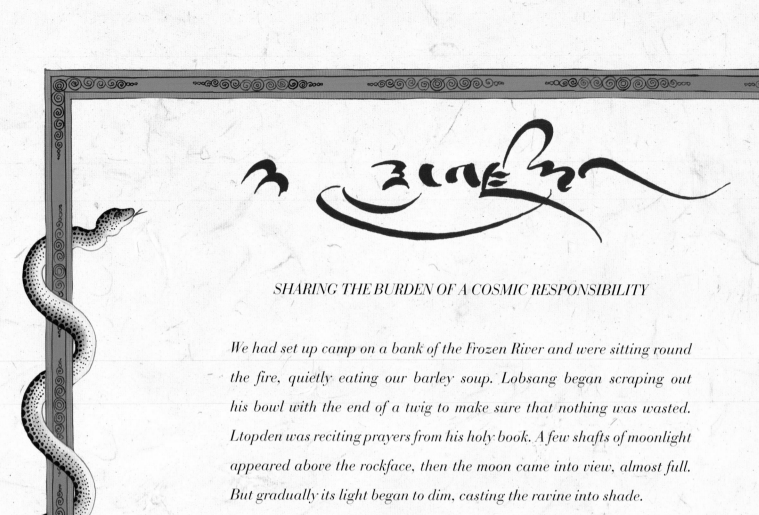

SHARING THE BURDEN OF A COSMIC RESPONSIBILITY

We had set up camp on a bank of the Frozen River and were sitting round the fire, quietly eating our barley soup. Lobsang began scraping out his bowl with the end of a twig to make sure that nothing was wasted. Ltopden was reciting prayers from his holy book. A few shafts of moonlight appeared above the rockface, then the moon came into view, almost full. But gradually its light began to dim, casting the ravine into shade.

'The moon!' cried Raften, pointing to the sky.

'Quick, they're going to eat the moon!' cried Ltopden.

Everyone began praying fervently, telling their rosaries with feverish hands as they watched the eclipse. From our firelit bank, the loud voices of the five men rose up towards the starry sky. The moon passed directly overhead, apparently half consumed. The prayers redoubled in their intensity, insistent and full of savage power. Slowly the earth's shadow moved on and the gorges leapt back into life. The prayers became murmers. The Zanskaris believe that during an eclipse there are animals eating the moon, and only the force of prayer can save it. On that particular evening gongs and cymbals were sounding in every monastery and chapel throughout Zanskar and monks and villagers were praying for the heavenly body to be saved.

The moon dipped out of sight below a rocky ridge. The fire was down to its embers, but the men were still praying, sharing the burden of a cosmic responsibility. Lobsang rose, climbed the slope towards the rocks and went to look at the moon. He came back, satisfied.

'The animals have stopped eating it.'

'What animals?'

'No one really knows; we think they are snakes.'

Thoughtfully, Lobsang went on: 'Olivier, couldn't the people from your country go up there and find out what animals they are?'

May the gods go with you

The river widened and the sheer rockfaces gradually gave way into shelving slopes of snow. Once again we could see into the distance. We were in Zanskar. On either side of the valley, the broad plateaux were whipped by winds from all directions. As we advanced, we had the sensation of walking on the spot: after being confined within the narrow gorge, we had forgotten what it was like to inhabit the open plain. It was so cold that the river steamed, the difference in temperature between the water under the ice and the air being something like 40°C (70°F). At sunset, the two precariously perched houses of Hanamur came into view. As we continued to blaze a trail though the snow, we were awestruck at the sight of these tiny islands of life. How could people live so far from the world? There were too many of us to stay in one house, so we split up. Lobsang knew the father at the upper house and agreed a price with him for wood.

In Zanskar the principal dwelling house is known as the *kampa*. When the elder son marries, his parents hand over the *kampa* to the young couple, with all the land attached to it. They themselves retire to the *kantchung*, a smaller and more simply furnished house near the *kampa*, where they take

⇜ Detail from a mural at
Karcha monastery.

⇜ Snowstorm on the
Frozen River.

a less active role. We were staying in the *kampa*. Five ragged children crouched beside us, staring, devouring with their eyes our cups of sweet tea. Uneasily, we chewed our lumps of frozen yak meat: we had forgotten the level of poverty in Zanskar. Hanamur was so remote, it received practically no visitors in winter and spring. Fortunately, the summer caravans passed right by the two houses, bringing a breath of life to these stranded children.

Two days later, we breasted the last ridge, where the *chörten* pointed ahead to the Tahan valley on the far side of a huge white snowfield. It had taken nearly two weeks' walking to get here, and it was a whole month since Lobsang had set out to meet us. Motup's eyes were shiny as the snow at the thought of seeing his mother Dolma, his sister Diskit and the two younger ones born during his long absence. With the stone prayer wall behind us, we peered ahead, as if to assure ourselves that the little house was still there, alone at the foot of the valley. In front of the narrow doorway on the low stone wall were two metal plates on which a few embers burned, mixed with pine needles. They had been placed there by Dolma in honour of our arrival, so that we could warm ourselves as she made the room ready. As we held our hands to the heat, we fell silent. The wooden door flew open and Dolma shot out, holding five silk scarves in her hand. Motup launched himself at her. 'Amale!' he cried. (*Ama* means mother; the suffix *le* implies respect.) Dolma placed a *katak* over her son's shoulder, then did the same for Danielle. Shaking with emotion, she fell into her arms and wept: words were redundant at such a moment. Diskit and her two small brothers were presiding over a big copper urn in the *yokhang*, full of pent-up excitement.

We spent ten days in Tahan, laughing, drinking and celebrating. Motup was the hero of the hour. He spoke four languages and could write three of them. Neighbours called in every day, installing themselves in the *yokhang* with the bottle of *arack* they had brought to celebrate our safe return.

They pored at length over the photos we had with us, photos of the school and that distant world from which we came. We related the story of our journey so many times we knew it by heart. Motup had to tell every visitor in turn about his life as a schoolboy, and Diskit pestered her brother to tell her in ten days all that he had experienced in three years. 'Atcho, from your school, can you see the moon?' Every evening we feasted on *moks-moks*, the local delicacy of ravioli made with goat's meat (the beast having been killed by a Muslim from Karcha, for Buddhists will never kill or imprison a living creature, not even the smallest of insects).

Motup's grandfather offered us a bowl of fresh blood from his goat, which he had bled specially for us. Dolma was radiant, so full of pride and happiness she could not take her eyes off her son. She herself had never been further than the monastery of Karcha, an hour's walk away. When, three years earlier, Lobsang had suggested sending their son away to school, Dolma had accepted the idea, trusting her husband. But there was no way she could have imagined the life he would lead. Three years on, she could see for herself how her boy was so much more grown up than any child from the locality. Motup could read, write and count, which neither she nor Lobsang could do. She was enthralled by the knowledge he had acquired, his disciplined attitude and his composure, and even the neighbours and the boy's grandfather were impressed by this child who had suddenly become the village sage. Yet Motup made light of his achievements. With typical Zanskari humility, he turned admiring comments into compliments to the others, insisting how much he had missed them.

Dolma was always the first to wake and on this particular morning she could be heard softly intoning a prayer; she ran her fingers through her hair and attached pieces of wool as extensions to her long black tresses, before donning a flame-coloured woollen bonnet. A little grey cat was sleeping on a coat, rolled in a ball against Diskit's cheek. The youngest of

The Zanskar Plain in January, seen from Stongde monastery, at 3,600 metres (11,800 feet).

Lobsang and Dolma happily reunited with their son Motup after three years.

HELPING THE WORLD TO ACHIEVE ENLIGHTENMENT

In Zanskar, you wait to cut your hair until there is a favourable moon. One day, Dorje was trying to cut Lobsang's hair with some huge scissors bartered from a Lahauli trader for two goatskins. As he removed each lock of hair, he placed it carefully between the dry stones of the wall. A few hairs fell in the snow and Lobsang leant over to pick them up and tuck them away in a crevice.

He saw that I was interested. 'You see,' he said, 'if you leave your hairs lying on the ground, the wet will turn them into insects. The life of insects is so brief that they have no time to fulfil themselves. It's a waste of a life for any being to be reincarnated as an insect in that way. If you put your hair, and horsehair too, in a dry place, you avoid that pointless reincarnation, and so help other beings to achieve Enlightenment more quickly.'

'Krampsang choste skiot! Go in peace', said the old man, and his beard shook as he spoke.

'Nyerang krampsang choste jux. Be in peace, Memele.'

Dolma took two tulle scarves from her *goncha* and turned to her son. With trembling hands, she placed a *katak* round his shoulders. Her voice was tearful.

'Ju Julley Ju, may the gods go with you....'

Motup held her hands, lowering his eyes and keeping his voice steady.

'Ju, Amale, Ju....'

Then Dolma turned to her daughter, placed a scarf around her shoulders and clasped her hands. The young girl did not move a muscle. When Dolma wished her happiness in a voice cracking with emotion, Diskit looked up at her with sparkling eyes. Why cry when you are being given the chance to go to school and follow your brother into a new world? Dolma continued to burrow in her *goncha*. She presented scarves to Lobsang and Norboo, then took out two more, weeping silently.

'Dany, Olivier, be happy. Take care of Motup and Diskit. I entrust my children to you: they are your children too.'

This baby is swaddled in a blanket lined with dried sheep dung, which serves as a nappy.

The journey to school. Motup helps his sister Diskit, for whom the Frozen River is a new experience.

The child needs the care of others to survive,
and love is his most important food.

His Holiness the fourteenth Dalai Lama

If you can keep your head when all about you
Are losing theirs and blaming it on you,
If you can trust yourself when all men doubt you,
But make allowance for their doubting too;
If you can wait and not be tired by waiting,
Or being lied about, don't deal in lies,
Or being hated, don't give way to hating,
And yet don't look too good, nor talk too wise:

If you can dream – and not make dreams your master;
If you can think – and not make thoughts your aim;
If you can meet with Triumph and Disaster
And treat those two imposters just the same;
If you can bear to hear the truth you've spoken
Twisted by knaves to make a trap for fools,
Or watch the things you gave your life to, broken,
And stoop and build 'em up with worn-out tools;

the temperature in the shade and that in the full sun was something approaching 45°C (80°F). Chahanchung stood like a beacon before us, the last house, the last island of life, before the Pensi La and the snowy ocean that lay beyond. Two women eked out a meagre existence there, at the foot of this remote valley, yet their energy and cheerfulness seemed to be unaffected by their isolation.

Crossing the Pensi La was an awesome experience. We allowed ourselves to be guided by the moon, murmering prayers that might have been echoing the music of the spheres. When the climb became steeper, two of us put on wooden crampons and gave the rest a hand. It was as if we were creeping with muffled footsteps towards the very brink of eternity. Before us lay the plateau leading to the pass, whose undulating snowy ridges rose and fell in wave after wave. Like some poor sea snake, our caravan advanced bravely from crest to crest.

The approaching dawn streaked the nearby summits with delicate shades of pastel. Looking back to the valleys of Zanskar slumbering in the shadowy distance, I felt overcome with emotion. Tears – the result of both sadness and the cold – froze on my eyelids as I joined my hands together and said a prayer. The peaks lit up one by one, the sky turned a deep blue, and the snowy slopes began to reverberate with light. The *karas* was becoming softer as the sunshine flooded in, and we found a spur of rock and laid down our bundles. All around us great plumes of vapour were blowing off the mountains into the blue sky. Our faces were burning as we ate some barley flour, leaning against a rock. In the middle of the day, when the snow reflected back the light with a ferocious intensity we could no longer endure, we fell asleep, like owls, in the shade.

While crossing the *karas*, faces and lips became painfully burnt by a combination of the cold and reflected sunlight.

The next day at dawn, we skirted Rangdum monastery, marooned on its hillside, then pressed on across the vast windswept plain to Parkachik,

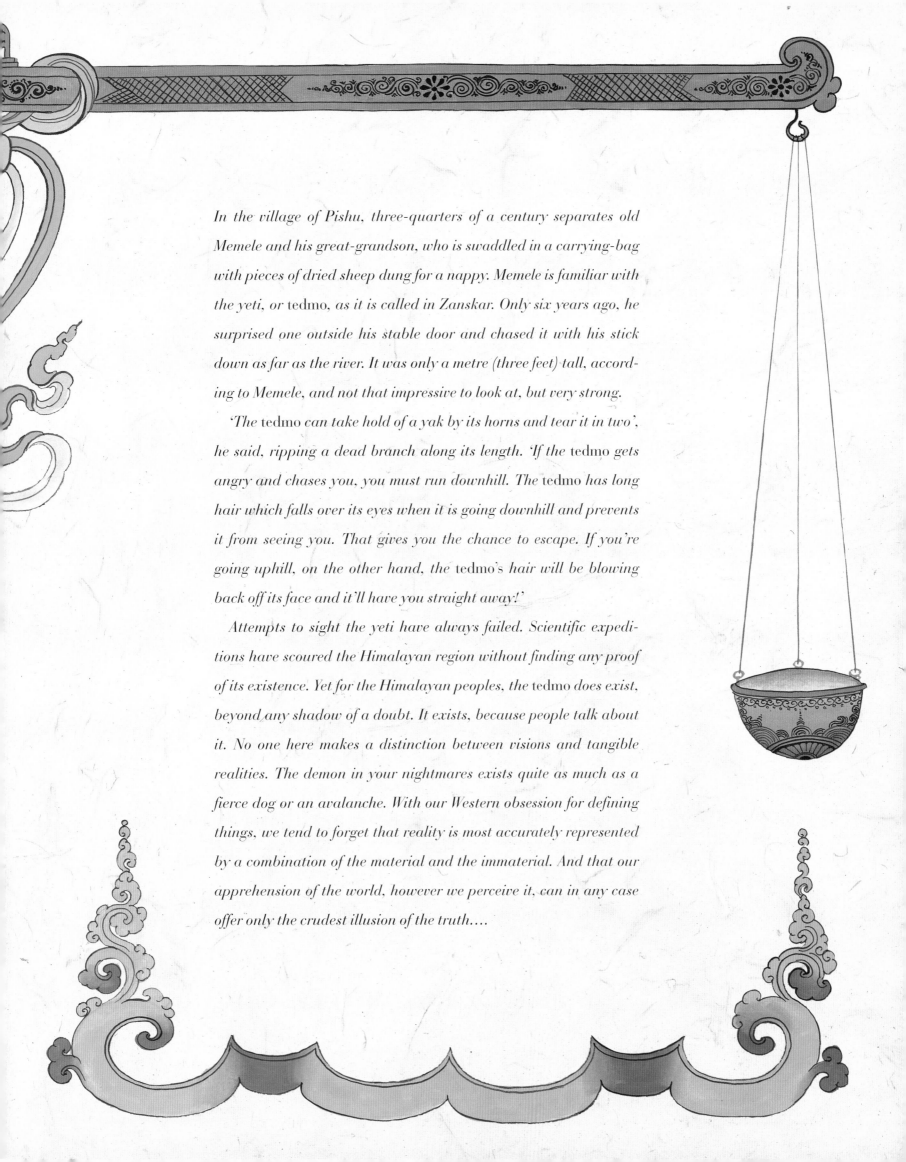

In the village of Pishu, three-quarters of a century separates old Memele and his great-grandson, who is swaddled in a carrying-bag with pieces of dried sheep dung for a nappy. Memele is familiar with the yeti, or tedmo, as it is called in Zanskar. Only six years ago, he surprised one outside his stable door and chased it with his stick down as far as the river. It was only a metre (three feet) tall, according to Memele, and not that impressive to look at, but very strong.

'The tedmo can take hold of a yak by its horns and tear it in two', he said, ripping a dead branch along its length. 'If the tedmo gets angry and chases you, you must run downhill. The tedmo has long hair which falls over its eyes when it is going downhill and prevents it from seeing you. That gives you the chance to escape. If you're going uphill, on the other hand, the tedmo's hair will be blowing back off its face and it'll have you straight away!'

Attempts to sight the yeti have always failed. Scientific expeditions have scoured the Himalayan region without finding any proof of its existence. Yet for the Himalayan peoples, the tedmo does exist, beyond any shadow of a doubt. It exists, because people talk about it. No one here makes a distinction between visions and tangible realities. The demon in your nightmares exists quite as much as a fierce dog or an avalanche. With our Western obsession for defining things, we tend to forget that reality is most accurately represented by a combination of the material and the immaterial. And that our apprehension of the world, however we perceive it, can in any case offer only the crudest illusion of the truth....

well prove fatal. The major factors are political tensions on its borders, the placing of garrisons in Ladakh, tourism and the growth of trade with India. The road has compounded the effect, by drawing people in from the plains: civil servants, tradesmen and travellers. At the same time it offers a window on the modern world to the younger generations of Zanskaris, numbers of whom can no longer tolerate the boredom of the long winter months and choose to go and work in Ladakh mending the roads. Some seek a more active and varied life by enlisting in the army, seeing the uniform as a mark of social status. They send their salaries back home, enabling their families to open up small shops in the villages. Diesel-generated electricity has appeared in three of the villages. Each home has the right to use two light bulbs. For many Zanskaris this has been nothing short of a miracle, and it has disposed them to look with favour on a modern world capable of such wonders. Must we therefore conclude that the minority culture of Zanskar is in terminal decline?

Nothing can survive unless it adapts – and that is as true of a people or a culture as it is of an individual. Change and growth are the essence of life. In the old days, the caravans used to arrive in summer to barter manufactured goods from the plains for wool and butter, which they could sell for a good price in the lower valleys. The Zanskaris became huge fans of the thermos flask and the pressure cooker, because they saved fuel. Next it was the metal cooking stove, lugged home on people's backs, which kept the winter room clear of smoke. The road may have put paid to the traditional caravans, but it has encouraged people to venture abroad. With the money gained from summer trade and tourism, many Zanskaris now go on pilgrimages to India and Nepal to visit the Buddhist holy places, and to pay homage to the Dalai Lama, their spiritual leader, in Dharmsala, on the southern tip of the Himalayas, where a Buddhist community lives in exile. The Dalai Lama regularly instructs monks and lay people all over the Himalayas. In Silliguri, for example, in 1996, he preached to 600,000